Jumpstarting Your New Team

Establishing Norms

Ken S. Keleman, Ph.D.

Pfeiffer
& COMPANY

Amsterdam • Johannesburg • Oxford
San Diego • Sydney • Toronto

Published by

Amsterdam
Pfeiffer & Company
Roggestraat 15
2153 GC Nieuw-Vennep
The Netherlands
31-2526-89840, FAX 31-2526-86885

Johannesburg
Pfeiffer & Company
P.O. Box 4684, Randburg, 2125
9 Langwa Street, Strijdom Park, Randburg, 2194
Republic of South Africa
27-11-792-8465/6/7, FAX 27-11-792-8046

Oxford
Pfeiffer & Company
27 Hanborough Business Park
Lodge Road
Long Hanborough, Witney
Oxfordshire OX8 8LH
England
44-99-388-3994, FAX 44-99-388-3996

San Diego
Pfeiffer & Company
8517 Production Avenue
San Diego, California 92121
United States of America
1-619-578-5900, FAX 1-619-578-2042

Sydney
Pfeiffer & Company
6/1 Short Street
Chatswood NSW 2067
Australia
61-2-417-5551, FAX 61-2-417-5621

Toronto
Pfeiffer & Company
4190 Fairview Street
Burlington, Ontario L7L 4Y8
Canada
1-416-632-5832, FAX 1-416-333-5675

Developmental Editing: *Carol Nolde*
Production Editing: *Dawn Kilgore*
Interior Design: *Judy Whalen*
Cover Art: *Lee Ann Hubbard*

CONTENTS

INTRODUCTION

Why Complete This Activity?

This activity is designed to help your team establish norms and get up to speed on its mission or task quickly. It also acquaints you and your fellow team members with critical individual behaviors that contribute to overall team effectiveness.

What Are Norms?

Norms are standards of conduct that regulate the behavior of the individual members of a team. These standards of conduct help the team members know how to function both within the team and outside it, with other organizational members, clients, and customers. Examples of norms are "Individual members should treat all team members as equals" and "Individual members should help other members when assistance is requested."

What Are the Benefits for My Team and Me?

Norms are a critical part of a team's life. Often they are established by accident (because of the initial behaviors of the original team members or because they are carried over from past work situations), less often by design. However, a team that consciously and purposefully sets its norms—especially at the beginning of its existence—enhances its chances for success in all of its efforts. When team members actively agree on how they want to function, they expedite many of their activities, such as problem solving and decision making, because they do not have to stop and wonder how to react when difficult situations arise (Hackman & Morris, 1975). Also, a team that has purposefully set norms can handle conflicts and disagreements more easily, because the pattern of response has been predetermined.

You will find that life in a team with norms that have been clearly established and are understood by all members is significantly easier and simpler than in a team without purposeful norms. There is no guesswork about day-to-day functioning—no wondering whether you have acted in a way that your supervisor and/or your fellow team members will find acceptable.

Hᴏᴡ ᴛᴏ ᴜꜱᴇ ᴛʜɪꜱ ᴀᴄᴛɪᴠɪᴛʏ

What Kind of Team Uses This Activity?

This activity is intended for an intact or ongoing work team, a self-directed work team, or a task force or project team that is functioning without a formal leader. It is best used when a team is just getting started, although it can also be beneficial for teams that have existed for some time.

Who Guides the Team Through the Activity?

The person chosen to guide your team through this activity is known as a *facilitator*. The facilitator may be the formal team leader (the supervisor), a team member, someone outside the team, or a professional trainer or consultant.

The facilitator's job is to assemble all necessary materials, to make sure that all steps of the process are completed in the manner prescribed in this booklet, to monitor the time required for each step, and to provide help (consultation, advice) if the team has difficulty completing any of the steps. In addition, if the facilitator is a member of the team, he or she should participate in the process, completing the steps along with the other members.

If the facilitator needs help in preparing to conduct the activity, he or she should consult the organization's human resource development department or representative or a supervisor who has experience in team leadership.

How Will We Decide on Norms?

To decide on norms, your team will use a technique called *consensus decision making*. A consensus decision is one that all team members can accept and live with, regardless of how satisfied they are with it. When striving for consensus, the team members actively seek and listen to everyone's opinion. Then there is discussion until consensus is reached. No "majority-rule" voting, bargaining, or averaging is allowed.

The value of consensus decision making lies in the fact that all of the team's resources are used; every member's ideas, feelings, and reactions are taken into consideration. Since all members will have to behave in accordance with the norms, it is important that every member has a say in choosing those norms. Only then can all members feel that they have been heard and their opinions honored, and only then can they feel that the norms truly belong to the team as a whole.

THE ACTIVITY PROCEDURE

Time Required

One hour and forty-five minutes to two hours.

Materials

1. One copy of *Jumpstarting Your New Team: Establishing Norms* for each team member.

2. A pencil or pen for each team member.

Physical Setting

A room in which the team members can work without being disturbed. A writing surface and a comfortable, movable chair should be provided for each team member. The team members should be seated so that they can see one another as well as the facilitator.

Step-by-Step Process

1. The facilitator gives each team member a copy of *Jumpstarting Your New Team: Establishing Norms* and a pencil or pen.

2. Each team member is asked to read the sections titled "Introduction" (page 1) and "How to Use This Activity" (page 2). (Ten minutes.)

3. The facilitator leads a brief discussion of what the team members have read, concentrating on how they will benefit from establishing norms. All team members are encouraged to participate in the discussion. (Ten minutes.)

4. The facilitator reviews Behavior List 1 (page 8) with the team, emphasizing that the behaviors on the list have been shown to discriminate between perceptions of effective and ineffective performance of team members (Spich & Keleman, 1985). The facilitator also explains that some behaviors may be considered *positive,* meaning that effective performance in the team is linked to *practicing* those behaviors, whereas some may be considered *negative,* meaning that effective performance is linked to *avoiding* those behaviors. (Ten minutes.)

5. Using the consensus method of decision making, the team members:

   • Decide which ten behaviors (whether positive or negative) have first priority or *are critical to the team's success* and mark those behaviors on page 8 with the letter "A";

   • Decide which ten behaviors have second priority or *are secondarily important to the team's success* and mark those behaviors on page 8 with the letter "B"; and

- Decide which ten behaviors have third priority or *should be paid attention to, but are not critically or secondarily important to the team's success,* and mark those behaviors on page 8 with the letter "C."

The facilitator declares the ten top-priority behaviors to be the team's norms. (If the team wishes, the ten second-priority behaviors may also be declared to be norms. More than twenty are generally too many to deal with.)

(Forty-five minutes to one hour.)

6. The facilitator leads a discussion by asking the following questions:

   - How did you feel about your fellow team members before participating in this activity? How do you feel about them now?

   - What is your reaction to the norms that the team established?

   - Which of these norms will be the most difficult for you to adhere to and why? How can your fellow team members help you to honor this norm?

   - How might adhering to the team's norms affect your personal contribution to the team?

   - What are some ideas for dealing with noncompliance to the team's norms?

   (Fifteen minutes.)

7. The facilitator reviews the section titled "The Importance of Follow-Up" on page 5 with the team members, emphasizing how critical it is to use feedback appropriately when norms are violated. Then the members read the section titled "Follow-Up Methods" on page 6 and decide which methods they want to use to reinforce their new norms. Any necessary follow-up plans are developed; if appropriate, arrangements are made to review the team's progress in adhering to its norms. (Fifteen minutes.)

VARIATIONS

1. To save time, the facilitator may distribute copies of *Jumpstarting Your New Team: Establishing Norms* several days in advance of the activity, asking the team members to read the sections titled "Introduction" and "How to Use This Activity" and to make notes on Behavior List 1 about personal behavioral preferences.

2. The team members may use Behavior List 2, which offers thirty additional behaviors connected with team effectiveness, in addition to Behavior List 1. If this variation is used, Step 5 under "Step-by-Step Process" will require another forty-five minutes to an hour.

3. The team members may add their own behaviors to Behavior List 1, including any behaviors related to unique situations and problems that they anticipate. These behaviors should be prioritized along with the ones already on the list. If this variation is used, Step 5 will require more time.

4. The team members may continue the activity by forming pairs and practicing giving and receiving feedback in a situation in which a team member has violated a team norm. (See the section titled "The Importance of Follow-Up.")

Follow-Up: Reinforcing and Reviewing Norms

The Importance of Follow-Up

Even the best intentions to act in accordance with team norms will not lead to agreed-on behavior unless the team makes plans for follow-up. You and your fellow team members must establish ways to reinforce and review norms, a way to inform new members of the team's norms, and a way to react when a member violates a norm.

The section titled "Follow-Up Methods" offers a number of suggestions on reinforcement and review. One excellent way to ensure that every person who joins the team learns the norms is to appoint another team member to serve as a "buddy" or a mentor for that person. The task of the buddy or mentor is to explain the norms and the team's expectations in detail.

When a team member violates a norm, you and the other members should call the behavior to the person's attention. Occasionally, too, a member may ask if he or she has acted appropriately, in accordance with a specific norm. Information regarding another person's behavior is known as *feedback*. Giving feedback intended to correct behavior is not easy, but it can be mastered with practice.

Following is some useful information on giving and receiving feedback:

Principles of Giving Feedback[*]

1. Give the feedback as soon after the behavior as possible, preferably immediately.

2. Deal with specific behavior, not generalities.

3. Describe the behavior that violated the norm; do not evaluate it. Never criticize or use punitive language.

4. Let the person know the impact that the behavior has on you.

5. Use an "I statement" to accept responsibility for your own observations, perceptions, and emotions.

6. Check to make sure that the person understood what you said in the way you intended.

    For example, assume that your team has decided all meetings will start on time. If one member arrives ten minutes late to a particular meeting, you might respond

---

[*]These principles and those on receiving feedback are adapted from "The Art of Feedback: Providing Constructive Information" by S.C. Bushardt and A.R. Fowler, Jr., 1989, in J.W. Pfeiffer (Ed.), *The 1989 Annual: Developing Human Resources* (p. 13), San Diego, CA: Pfeiffer & Company.

as follows: *"Chris, I noticed* ['I' statement] *that you arrived at the meeting at 10:10 instead of 10:00* [specific description of behavior and agreed-on norm]." Note that this statement does not evaluate the behavior or criticize Chris. Then you might continue by explaining the impact of Chris's late arrival on you: *"I feel* ['I' statement] *frustrated* [description of the emotion evoked] *because now we need to backtrack to fill you in on what we've already done* [explanation of cause of frustration]." Finally, you might say, *"Please let me know your understanding of the feedback I've just given you and what you think and feel about that feedback."* This kind of confrontation may seem awkward at first, but you and your fellow team members will grow used to it after a while.

Principles of Receiving Feedback

1. When you ask for feedback, be specific in describing the behavior about which you want the feedback.

2. Try not to act defensively or rationalize your behavior. Thank the person for the feedback.

3. Summarize your understanding of the feedback that you receive.

4. Share your thoughts and feelings about the feedback.

    For example, assume again that your team has decided all meetings will start on time. You have been having difficulty with this particular commitment, and you want feedback about your arrival at recent meetings. You might ask a fellow team member, *"In the past week* [specific time period], *how have I been doing on getting to meetings on time* [specific behavior]?" Then another team member might say, "I noticed that you arrived a few minutes late for Tuesday's meeting, but you were on time for the meetings on Wednesday and Thursday." An appropriate response on your part would be *"Thanks for the feedback. I understand that you noticed I was a few minutes late once and on time twice* [summary of the feedback]. *I feel good about being on time twice* [sharing feelings about the feedback], *and maybe next week will go even better."*

Follow-Up Methods

1. Your team may post its final list of norms prominently in its usual meeting room.

2. You and your fellow team members may monitor members' behavior during team meetings: Appoint one member to monitor for several meetings or several weeks; then switch to another member. Rotate the responsibility of monitoring at least every few weeks so that all members have a chance to monitor. The appointed monitor reports on behavioral consistency with norms at the end of each meeting. (Refer to the Sample Meeting-Evaluation Sheet on page 12. Your team may use this evaluation sheet as a model to construct one of its own, using norms that would be particularly relevant to behavior in

meetings. Note that any form used must be simple enough to complete so that the monitor can participate in the meeting as well as fulfill the monitoring responsibility.)

3. Your team may review the list of norms periodically, altering norms if necessary due to changes in team responsibilities, structure, processes, or membership.

4. The members of your team may form pairs for contracting purposes. One member contracts with another so that the two can help each other with norms that they find troublesome. The contracting partners serve as monitors and coaches, encouraging each other. (Refer to the Sample Contract on page 11.)

5. The facilitator or all team members working together may construct an assessment form to evaluate each member's adherence to norms. (See the Sample Assessment Form on page 10.) All norms assigned "A" and "B" priority (or any number of norms) may be used. Each team member completes the form on every team member, including himself or herself. The form is filled out periodically throughout the life of the team; the results are shared and discussed; and the form or the team norms are adjusted as necessary. If the facilitator needs help in constructing the assessment form, he or she should check with the organization's human resource representative or department.

REFERENCES AND BIBLIOGRAPHY

Bushardt, S.C., & Fowler, A.R., Jr. (1989). The art of feedback: Providing constructive information. In J.W. Pfeiffer (Ed.), *The 1989 annual: Developing human resources* (pp. 9-16). San Diego, CA: Pfeiffer & Company.

Hackman, J.R., & Morris, C.G. (1975). Group tasks, group interaction processes, and group performance: A review and proposed integration. In L. Berkowitz (Ed.), *Advances in Experimental and Social Psychology,* Vol. 8, pp. 45-99. San Diego, CA: Academic Press.

Kormanski, C., & Mozenter, A. (1987). A new model of team building: A technology for today and tomorrow. In J.W. Pfeiffer (Ed.), *The 1987 annual: Developing human resources* (pp. 255-268). San Diego, CA: Pfeiffer & Company.

Robbins, S.P. (1992). *Essentials of organizational behavior* (3rd ed.). Englewood Cliffs, NJ: Prentice-Hall.

Sherwood, J.J., & Glidewell, J.C. (1973). Planned renegotiation: A norm-setting OD intervention. In J.E. Jones & J.W. Pfeiffer (Eds.), *The 1973 annual handbook for group facilitators* (pp. 195-202). San Diego, CA: Pfeiffer & Company.

Solomon, L.N. (1977). Team development: A training approach. In J.E. Jones & J.W. Pfeiffer (Eds.), *The 1977 annual handbook for group facilitators* (pp. 181-193). San Diego, CA: Pfeiffer & Company.

Spich, R.S., & Keleman, K.S. (1985). Explicit norm structuring process: A strategy for increasing task-group effectiveness. *Group & Organization Studies, 10*(1), 37-59.

Behavior List 1[*]

While working in our team, individuals should...

1. Do their fair share of the work.
2. Check to ensure that everyone clearly understands what is to be done.
3. Be clear and concise in their communication.
4. Encourage planning, including short-range agendas as well as long-range goals.
5. Encourage open and candid opinions about issues.
6. Listen willingly and carefully to other people's ideas, even if those people have a different viewpoint.
7. Prepare thoroughly before meetings.
8. Help the team organize work, for example, delegate assignments.
9. Make team members feel at ease in discussions.
10. Involve others by asking questions.
11. Ask questions when they do not clearly understand tasks or procedures.
12. Propose specific analyses of the pros and cons of decisions faced by the team.
13. Follow through on task assignments.
14. Be grouchy and grumpy, complaining about tasks, working conditions, etc.
15. Help other members when assistance is requested.
16. Restate or clarify the team's objectives if the team seems to drift off target.
17. Treat all team members as equals.
18. Paraphrase or restate what someone else says in order to check meaning.
19. Let personal differences with other members interfere with team activity.
20. Continue to look for different ways to solve a problem.
21. Openly voice opinions and share ideas.
22. Request a response from each team member before making a decision about a team issue.
23. Be flexible in arranging meeting schedules.
24. Ask about other people's feelings.
25. Be stubborn and unwilling to listen to the ideas of others.
26. Compliment others for things they have said or done.
27. Openly enjoy working in the team.
28. Be willing to meet whenever it is necessary to discuss a problem.
29. Respond to suggestions.
30. Make rude remarks.

---

*From "Explicit Norm Structuring Process: A Strategy for Increasing Task-Group Effectiveness" by R.S. Spich & K.S. Keleman, 1985, in *Group & Organization Studies, 10*(1), 37-59. Adapted with permission. A discussion of the development of the items in the list can be found in this article.

Behavior List 2[*]

While working in our team, individuals should...

1. Deal with conflict directly, bringing it to the attention of the team.
2. Express enthusiasm about what the team is doing.
3. Promote personal agendas over the team's concerns.
4. Promote brainstorming sessions before choosing a solution.
5. Criticize other members' ideas without offering alternatives.
6. Be sarcastic or make fun of ideas presented.
7. Encourage budgeting of the team's time.
8. At the end of a meeting, restate their own responsibilities to check for agreement.
9. Meet agreed-on deadlines.
10. Be serious about the team's work.
11. Watch the clock.
12. Deliver poor-quality work.
13. Make critical comments about other team members in their absence.
14. Interrupt other members while they are speaking.
15. Make negative comments about ideas presented ("That's dumb!").
16. Arrive on time for regularly scheduled meetings.
17. Do little things to make it pleasant to be a member of the team.
18. Talk about topics that do not relate to the subject at hand.
19. Be willing to listen to other team members' ideas.
20. Put off work until a later time (procrastinate).
21. Encourage the team to review its accomplishments to date.
22. Constantly pick fights and bicker with other members.
23. Say "Let's not adjourn the meeting until we have a firm grasp of the problem."
24. Disagree in a nice way.
25. Get the team's approval on important matters before proceeding.
26. Say "Thank you" and offer compliments.
27. Play around and joke when the team is trying to get something done.
28. Be direct and accurate in expressing their own feelings; say what they feel.
29. Encourage the assignment of specific members to do particular jobs.
30. Agree just for the sake of putting an end to an issue.

---

[*]From "Explicit Norm Structuring Process: A Strategy for Increasing Task-Group Effectiveness" by R.S. Spich & K.S. Keleman, 1985, in *Group & Organization Studies, 10*(1), 37-59. Adapted with permission. A discussion of the development of the items in the list can be found in this article.

Sample Assessment Form[*]

Instructions: Evaluate the behavior of each person on your team, including yourself, by completing a copy of this form. For each behavior, place an "X" in the column that most accurately describes how frequently the person you are rating engages in that behavior. For example, if "Becomes sidetracked with small talk" were a behavior you observed *often*, then you would place an "X" in the column labeled "Often."

This person...

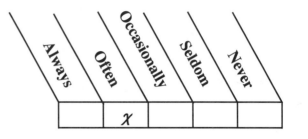

1. Openly enjoys working in the team.

——— Please respond to all items ———

The team member I am rating is:

Chris Johnson

This person...

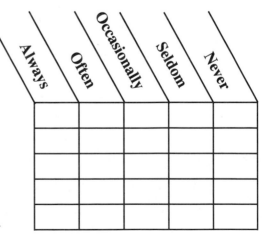

1. Does his or her fair share of the work.

2. Disagrees in a nice way.

3. Arrives on time for regularly scheduled meetings.

4. Encourages budgeting of the team's time.

5. Interrupts other members while they are speaking.

[*]From "Explicit Norm Structuring Process: A Strategy for Increasing Task-Group Effectiveness" by R.S. Spich & K.S. Keleman, 1985, in *Group & Organization Studies, 10*(1), 37-59. Adapted with permission.

Sample Contract Form

We, the undersigned, agree to help each other adhere to the following team norms:

1. **Arrive on time for regularly scheduled meetings.**

   For the next three months, from September 1 through November 30, we will:

   - Get together every Monday at 9:00 a.m. to get clear on what meetings we have to attend during the week. We will record these meetings in our daily-reminder records or on our calendars.

   - Call each other fifteen minutes before the time of each meeting and remind each other not to get involved in anything in the next fifteen minutes that might make us late for the meeting.

   - Get together every Friday at 4:00 p.m. to review how we did that week on getting to meetings on time.

   At the end of the three-month period, we will decide whether to continue or change our plan for helping each other.

2. **Disagree in a nice way.**

   For the next three months, from September 1 through November 30, we will:

   - Monitor each other's behavior during team meetings to check for examples of disagreeing in a nice way and in an unacceptable way. After each team meeting we will meet for five minutes to share feedback and suggestions with each other.

   - Compliment each other when we hear ourselves disagreeing appropriately in conversations with others (outside meetings); call it to each other's attention when we hear ourselves disagreeing inappropriately.

   At the end of the three-month period, we will decide whether to continue or change our plan for helping each other.

   Signature _____ Date _____

   Signature _____ Date _____

Sample Meeting-Evaluation Sheet

Instructions: During the team meeting, monitor the members' interactions and complete this sheet. For each item, put a check mark in the appropriate blank. Jot down remarks in the "Notes and Comments" section, and be sure to give the team feedback at the end of the meeting.

	Always	Often/As often as possible	Seldom/Not as often as possible	Never
During the meeting the team members:				
1. Were clear and concise in their communication.	_____	_____	_____	_____
2. Listened willingly and carefully to other people's ideas, even when those people had a different viewpoint.	_____	_____	_____	_____
3. Asked questions when they did not clearly understand tasks or procedures.	_____	_____	_____	_____
4. Involved others by asking questions.	_____	_____	_____	_____
5. Were grouchy and grumpy, complaining about tasks, working conditions, etc.	_____	_____	_____	_____
6. Treated all team members as equals.	_____	_____	_____	_____
7. Paraphrased or restated what someone else said in order to check meaning.	_____	_____	_____	_____
8. Openly voiced opinions and shared ideas.	_____	_____	_____	_____
9. Asked about other people's feelings.	_____	_____	_____	_____
10. Expressed enthusiasm about what the team was doing.	_____	_____	_____	_____

Notes and Comments: